Warning To The Muslims

The Quran Is Coming
White Privilege Is Done

By Rasheed L. Muhammad

Forward

This book *"Warning To The Muslims: The Quran Is Coming: White Privilege is Done"* provides a few Quranic Reminder (verses) to stimulate the upright thinking within both man and women. Many do not know nor understand how we are all living under the influence of the Adamic civilization. In other words, the world dominated by white privilege that was given 6,000 years to govern humanity using all manner of evil, mischief and immorality i.e., Satan.

The Holy Quran is the voice of instructions of our ancestors who once ruled far beyond 6,000 years ago, in righteousness. By writing and releasing portions of the Holy Quran, their intention was that it be applied to relieve humanity from suffering from the destructive side of humanities nature or desires, wants and needs when he or she cannot get our way.

"Warning To The Muslims: The Quran Is Coming: White Privilege is Done" includes verses, Reminder or passages taken from the Holy Quran's interpreted by Maulana Muhammad Ali and Yusuf Ali. These two scholars provide the best English versions to read.

After reading the various Quranic Reminder (verses or passages) contained in this book, it compels our nature to think about today's society, our own lives, past and present. It wakes us up to see what human beings have done and are currently doing wrong to self and others; no matter what religion is declared. Because the Holy Quran deals with living human beings, what you shall read at times will make you happy, sad, upset, and ashamed. Why? Our nature inclines from one side (good) to the other side (other than good). So without Divine law applied to govern our nature in society, hell erupts as seen in every nation on earth.

I reiterate, the Holy Quran is the voice of instructions of our ancient ancestors whom all bowed down to A*lll*ah—God's wisdom. Unfortunately, over past 6,000 years, the satanic way of life established under *White Privilege* is dominating Black America. Subsequently, we, descendants of the ancients, are the worst victims to all sorts of evil, mischief and immorality.

By not knowing, reading or rejecting the Holy Quran's social order, business ethics, proper sexual intercourse, family inheritance rules, moral codes, marriage courtship, and affairs of self-defense; just to name of few, much pain and deviant behaviors have been passed down from parent to child, from church to church-goer to long for us to remember. The A*lll*ah of the Holy Quran condemns child molestation, rape, drunkenness, beating your women, stealing, adultery by men or women, prostitution, pimping, burglary, unjust murder, eating bad foods for your health, smoking, gambling, low wage pay and loving your enemies. If you take notice, all of these social deviations are against human nature, yet practiced by humans under a world dominated by White Privilege.

What is White Privilege that it has created so much rebellion against A*lll*ah and the Holy Quran? According to Peggy McIntosh, whites in a Western societies enjoy advantages that non-whites do not experience, as "an invisible package of unearned assets"…White privilege (or white skin privilege) is a term for societal privileges that benefit people identified as white in Western countries, beyond what is commonly experienced by non-white people under the same social, political, or economic circumstances. Academic perspectives such as critical race theory and whiteness studies use the concept of "white privilege" to analyze how racism and radicalized societies affect the lives of white or white-skinned people.[1]

---

[1] McIntosh, Peggy. "Unpacking the Invisible Knapsack." Beyond Heroes and Holidays. 1998. Endid Lee. Teaching for Change, 1998.

So you ask the question who is Alllah? Alllah is The True and Living God! When the name Alllah is said, that does not mean the same word as Allah spelled with two letter L's. **Allah** with two letter L's merely means **deity**—a non-living object of worship. Its spelling A-L-L-A-H with two letter L's is a "white" Arabized spelling to satisfy the European concept of god because the European language (English) could not see a reason to include 3 letters L's as it is employed in the more ancient Arabic spelling—Alllah.

So the actual and more ancient name and spelling is Alllah spelled with 3 letter L's. Alllah is not the title of a deity (god). Alllah is not a contraction. His name engulfs much linguistical unlimited divine meaning. Alllah is a Man or He! Alllah is the Original Black Nation of Asia (Ancestors to us all).

"Even as We produced the first creation, so shall We produce a new one; a promise We have undertaken. Truly shall We fulfill it." (21:104)

Alllah is self-created and has created us from a single cell right down to these modern times. To properly understand Alllah will clearly tell us this Name is older than the Arabic language itself being derived from a former and more ancient language which constituted such a grammatical character which does not exist in the Arabic Language as we know it today with any other word.[2]

Therefore, when Alllah is mentioned henceforth, it does not refer to a spook or ghost floating around somewhere or anywhere in space. Alllah is The Divine Supreme Being. Our divine ancestors did not leave us alone.

---

[2] http://allahumma.blogspot.com/

"We have, without doubt, sent down the Message; and We will assuredly guard it (from corruption)." (Holy Quran 15: 9)

It is from this Divine Circle Human Beings from whence the Holy Quran's messages were revealed over one thousand years ago that we might be guided in accordance to our nature and act it out with just means. As you will see, the societal problems that existed thousands of years ago, yet exist today especially by youth. For without Divine guidance, youth and young adults often become servants of the lowest desires in name of having fun, sport and play.

In summary, the Holy Quran consists of prophecies written for us today. It also contains many allegorical histories (stories in which people and events have a symbolic meaning) such as those about Prophet Abraham, Moses, Jesus and the like. However, this book *"Warning To The Muslims: The Quran Is Coming: White Privilege is Done"* will not delve into those allegories. It deals with those elements giving people the ability to make decisions or something that determines what comes next concerning how we will clean up our own life and community until another Quran is revealed to get us over into the life of the Hereafter.

"Ha Mim By the Book that makes things clear,- We have made it a Quran in Arabic that you may be able to understand. And verily, it is the Mother of the Book with us, (high) in dignity full of wisdom. Shall We then turn away from the Reminder altogether, for you are a people transgressing beyond bounds?" (Holy Quran 43:2-5)

Prologue

Black people of America, who will agree, truly need some land to call their own. As early as 1934, the Honorable Elijah Muhammad stated:

"We want our people in America whose parents or grandparents were descendants from slaves, to be allowed to establish a separate state or territory of their own–either on this continent or elsewhere. We believe that our former slave masters are obligated to provide such land and that the area must be fertile and minerally rich. We believe that our former slave masters are obligated to maintain and supply our needs in this separate territory for the next 20 to 25 years–until we are able to produce and supply our own needs.

"Since we cannot get along with them in peace and equality, after giving them 400 years of our sweat and blood and receiving in return some of the worst treatment human beings have ever experienced, we believe our contributions to this land and the suffering forced upon us by white America, justifies our demand for complete separation in a state or territory of our own."[3]

Overall, Black America's social problems and transgressions beyond bounds must be addressed by what Alllah has set forth in the Holy Quran and not legal fiction which is: a rule assuming as true something that is clearly false. A fiction is often used to get around the provisions of constitutions and legal codes that legislators are hesitant to change or to encumber with specific limitations. Thus, when a legislature has no legal power to sit beyond a certain midnight but has five hours more of work still to do, it is easier to turn back the official clock from time to time than it is to change the law or constitution.[4]

---

[3] http://www.noi.org/muslim-program/
[4] http://www.britannica.com/topic/legal-fiction

Either U.S. law or the constitution has failed Black America or Black America failed U.S. law and the constitution. Again, either way, the question is: is it time for Black people to govern themselves as a nation, state or territory?

What is the difference between a state, territory and a nation? Well, the concept of a **"nation,"** refers to a large geographical area, and the people therein who **perceive themselves as having a common identity Government is broadly defined as the administrative group of people with authority to govern a political state**.

A "**state**" is **an organized community living under a unified political system, the government.** Every State consists of "**cities**". Every citizen should engage in **civic duties**. Some say the duties of good citizens are not easy to determine. So what duties are we talking about? Well every citizen of any good government is taught how to be organized and responsible in his/her conscience, taught the laws of his/her nation and trained to be family and community oriented. This is achieved by being informed how to contribute to your society. **Civic means**, *"of, relating to, or belonging to a city, a citizen, or citizenship, municipal or civil society."*[5]

Lastly, a Territory is: a geographic area belonging to or under the jurisdiction of a governmental authority *b*: an administrative subdivision of a country *c*: a part of the United States or other Country not included within any state but organized with a separate legislature *d*: a geographic area (as a colonial possession) dependent on an external government but having some degree of autonomy.

The following Quranic passage is actually about members of the Lost and Found Nation of Islam in the West and the Jewish people. At some point and time, a

[5] "Transition of Nations: A Time For Universal Change" By Wahid Muhammad and Rasheed L Muhammad pages 38-39.

real relationship shall be established and a nation will be born without interference from neither fools, agents nor provocateurs.

"*You have been the best nation that has been raised up for men. You enjoin what is right, forbid what is wrong, and believe in Allah. If the People of the Book believe [in Islam], it would be better for them; there are believers among them, but most of them are backsliders. They will not harm you but a slight hurt. If they fight you, they shall turn their backs to you [to flee], and they shall not be helped. Abasement has been imposed on them wherever they are found, except under a covenant with Allah and a covenant with men, and they have become deserving of wrath from Allah, and humiliation is made to cleave to them. This is because they disbelieved in the verses of Allah and slew the prophets unjustly. This is because they disobeyed and exceeded the limits. They are not all alike; among the People of the Book there is an upright party; they recite Allah's verses in the nighttime, falling prostrate. They believe in Allah and the Last Day, they enjoin what is right and forbid what is wrong, and they hasten to good works. Those are among the righteous. Whatever good they do, they shall not be denied it. Allah knows the devout.*" (Holy Quran 3:110-115)

Rasheed L Muhammad

January 25, 2016

Quranic Reminder Concerning Government Representatives and Prophets are not Dictators

1. "So whatever you are given is but a provision of this world's life, and that which Allah has is better and more lasting for those who believe and rely on their Lord; And those who shun the great sins and indecencies, and whenever they are angry they forgive; And those who respond to their Lord and keep up prayer, and whose affairs are (decided) by counsel among themselves, and who spend out of what We have given them; And those who, when great wrong afflicts them, defend themselves." (Holy Quran Chapter 42 verse 36-39)

2. "Thus it is by Allah's mercy that thou art gentle to them. And hadst thou been rough, hard-hearted, they would certainly have dispersed from around thee. So pardon them and ask protection for them, and consult them in (important) matters. But when thou hast determined, put thy trust in Allah. Surely Allah loves those who trust (in Him). If Allah helps you, there is none that can overcome you; and if He forsakes you, who is there that can help you after Him? And in Allah should the believers put their trust. And it is not for a prophet to act dishonestly. And whoever acts dishonestly will bring his dishonesty on the day of Resurrection. Then shall every soul be paid back fully what it has earned, and they will not be wronged. Is then he who follows the pleasure of Allah like him who incurs Allah's displeasure,

and his abode is hell? And it is an evil destination." (Holy Quran Chapter 3 verse 159-161)

THE BOSSES OF THE SENATE.

* The role of the military-industrial complex is hardly new – as this 19th century cartoon exemplifies. Isn't it time we really tackled it? Over to you, taxpayers.[6]

Questions to think about: *Of course age and life experiences may limit how one understands and accepts the way of life Alllah set forth for us living in the current Adamic civilization ruled under "white privilege".*

---

[6] http://wellthisiswhatithink.com/2013/07/13/defence-spending/

- Do you belong to a governing body or counsel of men and women who decide the affairs of others?
- What government has mistreated Black America roughly and unjustly?
- What does Alllah mean by "*shun the great sins and indecencies?*"
- What is a Trust in terms of big business and its sins?
- How does Alllah set-forth some general principles for government authorities (counsels of men and women) to apply when ruling over people?
- Are Corporations like governments run by counsels of men and women?

Quranic Reminder Concerning Social Responsibility Toward Parents, Relatives and Neighbors

3. "Your Sustainer has decreed that you worship none but Him, and that you be kind to parents. Whether one or both of them attain old age in your lifetime, do not say to them a word of contempt nor repel them, but address them in terms of honor. And, out of kindness, lower to them the wing of humility and say: My Sustainer! Bestow on them Your mercy, even as they cherished me in childhood. Your Lord knows best what is in your minds. If you are righteous, He is surely Forgiving to those who turn (to Him). And give to the near of kin his due and (to) the needy and the wayfarer, and squander not wastefully. Surely the squanderers are the devil's brethren. And the devil is ever ungrateful to his Lord." (Chapter 17 verses 23-24)

4. "And render to the relatives their due rights, as (also) to those in need, and to the traveler; and do not squander your wealth in the manner of a spendthrift. And if you [must] turn away from the needy awaiting mercy from your Lord which you expect, then speak to them a gentle word. And do not make your hand [as] chained to your neck or extend it completely and [thereby] become blamed and insolvent." (Chapter 17: verse 26-30)

Questions to think about: *Of course age and life experiences may limit how one understands and accepts the way of life Alllah set forth for us living in the current Adamic civilization ruled under "white privilege".*

- Do you squander—recklessly and extravagantly consume material products?
- How has today's world order negatively affected child to parent relationships and raised squanderers?
- How do government officials squander the wealth of society?
- What is a spendthrift and how can this Quranic passive make one aware that wealth can be rightly used to assist relatives, the needy, neighbors self and socialites progress?

Quranic Reminder Concerning Morals Over Legalities

5. "It is not righteousness that you turn your faces towards East or West; but it is righteousness to believe in God and the Last Day and the Angels, and the Book, and the Messengers; to spend of your substance, out of love for Him, for your kin,

for orphans for the needy, for the wayfarer, for those who ask; and for the freeing of captives; to be steadfast in prayers, and practice regular charity; to fulfill the contracts which you made; and to be firm and patient in pain (or suffering) and adversity and throughout all periods of panic. Such are the people of truth, the God-conscious." (Chapter 2 verse 177)

6. "And hasten to forgiveness from your Lord and a garden (*Paradise*) as wide as the heavens and the earth, prepared for the righteous. Who spend (*in the cause of Allah*) during ease and hardship and who restrain anger and who pardon the people – and Allah loves the doers of good." (Quran: 3:133-134)

Questions to think about: *Of course age and life experiences may limit how one understands and accepts the way of life Alllah set forth for us living in the current Adamic civilization ruled under "white privilege".*

- How has today's world order set forth obstacles for helping to free wrongly convicted prisoners, helping orphans, single mothers, and poor people?
- Do single provisions of law, corrupted lawyers, racist customs, court systems and self-righteousness people dominate this world order?
- How can the Quranic passage 2:177 bring a change to the fundamental principles of righteousness, moral conduct over legalities and corrupt laws if legislated into due process of law?
- What is God-conscious?
- What amount of investment is needed to overturn corruption?

- Why would lack of money prevent you from spending money to assist spreading righteousness rather than filth, evil and drunkenness?
- What moral obligation or role does government play to work for the good of its citizens since governments collect taxes from its citizens?

Quranic Reminder Concerning God-Consciousness

7. "The most honorable among you in the sight of God is the one who is most God-conscious." (Chapter 49 verse 13)

8. "Establish regular prayer, enjoin what is just, and forbid what is wrong; and bear patiently whatever may befall you; for this is true constancy. And do not swell your cheek (with pride) at men, nor walk in insolence on the earth, for God does not love any man proud and boastful. And be moderate in your pace and lower your voice; for the harshest of sounds, indeed, is the braying of the ass." (Chapter 31 verses 18-19)

9. "Those who believe, and whose hearts find satisfaction in the remembrance of Allah: for without doubt in the remembrance of Allah do hearts find satisfaction. (Holy Quran Chapter 13 verse 28)

Questions to think about: *Of course age and life experiences may limit how one understands and accepts the way of life Alllah set forth for us living in the current Adamic civilization ruled under "white privilege".*

- How does God-Consciousness gain strength within you?

- How is God-Consciousness manifested from man/woman to community and government?
- Why do Alllah hate braggers and disrespectful people?

Quranic Reminder Concerning How To Properly Divorce and Not Abuse Women During Breakups

10. "O you who believe, it is not lawful for you to take women as heritage against (their) will. Nor should you straiten them by taking part of what you have given them, unless they are guilty of manifest indecency. And treat them kindly. Then if you hate them, it may be that you dislike a thing while Allah has placed abundant good in it. And if you wish to have (one) wife in the place of another and you have given one of them a heap of gold, take nothing from it. Would you take it by slandering (her) and (doing her) manifest wrong?" (Holy Quran Chapter 4 verses 19-20)

11. "Those who swear that they will not go in to their wives should wait four months; then if they go back, Allah is surely Forgiving, Merciful. And if they resolve on a divorce, Allah is surely Hearing, Knowing. And the divorced women should keep themselves in waiting for three courses. And it is not lawful for them to conceal that which Allah has created in their wombs, if they believe in Allah and the Last Day. And their husbands have a better right to take them back in the meanwhile if they wish for reconciliation. And women have rights similar to those against them in a just manner, and men are a degree above them. And

Allah is Mighty, Wise." (Holy Quran Chapter 2 verses 226-228)

Questions to think about: *Of course age and life experiences may limit how one understands and accepts the way of life Alllah set forth for us living in the current Adamic civilization ruled under "white privilege".*

- What is open illegal sexual intercourse and manifest indecency?
- Do you know anyone who takes his wife's money by force?
- What is a pimp?
- What has Alllah commanded men not to do which constitutes mistreatment women?
- What does Alllah mean by saying "men are one degree above them"—i.e., women?

Quranic Reminder Concerning Muslim Dress Code

"Say to the believing men that they lower their gaze and restrain their sexual passions. That is purer for them. Surely Allah is Aware of what they do. And say to the believing women that they lower their gaze and restrain their sexual passions and do not display their adornment except what appears thereof. And let them wear their head-coverings over their bosoms. And they should not display their adornment except to their husbands or their fathers, or the fathers of their husbands, or their sons, or the sons of their husbands, or their brothers, or their brothers' sons, or their sisters' sons, or their women, or those whom their right hands possess, or guileless male servants, or the children who know not women's nakedness. And let them not strike their feet so that the adornment that they hide may be known.

And turn to Allah all, O believers, so that you may be successful." (Holy Quran Chapter 24 verse 30-31)

Clothed by "shameless"
Message of freedom

Clothed by Alllah's
Message of freedom

Questions to think about: *Of course age and life experiences may limit how one understands and accepts the way of life Alllah set forth for us living in the current Adamic civilization ruled under "white privilege".*

- What is the motivation behind a women wearing tight fitting close?
- As a man what do you think and see women in tight fitting pants. As a women what comes to your mind when you wear revealing clothes in public?
- Why has Alllah—The God set forth a standard for women to not display their full beauty in public?
- How do you want your mother, sister or daughter to dress in public?

Quranic Reminder Concerning Sin of Incest And Sex With Relatives.

12. "And marry not women whom your fathers married, except what has already passed. This surely is indecent and hateful; and it is an evil way. Forbidden to you are your mothers, and your daughters, and your sisters, and your paternal aunts, and your maternal aunts, and brother's daughters and sister's daughters, and your mothers that have suckled you, and your foster-sisters, and mothers of your wives, and your stepdaughters who are in your guardianship (born) of your wives to whom you have gone in — but if you have not gone in to them, there is no blame on you — and the wives of your sons who are of your own loins; and that you should have two sisters together, except what has already passed. Surely Allah is ever Forgiving, Merciful, And all married women except those whom your right hands possess (are forbidden); (this is) Allah's ordinance to you. And lawful for you are (all women) besides those, provided that you seek (them) with your property, taking (them) in marriage, not committing fornication. Then as to those whom you profit by (by marrying), give them their dowries as appointed. And there is no blame on you about what you mutually agree after what is appointed (of dowry). Surely Allah is ever Knowing, Wise." (Holy Quran Chapter 24 verse 22-24)

Questions to think about: _Of course age and life experiences may limit how one understands and accepts the way of life Alllah set forth for us living in the current Adamic civilization ruled under "white privilege"._

- How do all of the above unrefined human practices destroy women, children and society at large?
- Why does Alllah say marry women before having sex—fornicating?
- Are you more knowing and wiser after learning from your mistakes?

Quranic Reminder Concerning Unclean Sex With A Wife

13. "And they ask thee about menstruation. Say: It is harmful, so keep aloof from women during menstrual discharge and go not near them until they are clean. But when they have cleansed themselves, go in to them as God has commanded you. Surely God loves those who turn much (to Him), and He loves those who purify themselves. Your wives are a tilth for you, so go in to your tilth when you like, and send (good) beforehand for yourselves. And keep your duty to God, and know that you will meet Him. And give good news to the believers." (Holy Quran 2 verse 222)

*Menstruation (period) sex is forbidden in the Islamic world to avoid (a) optimum risk of infections, (b) susceptible vulvar skin irritation; (c) menstrual blood can also dilute the effects of both natural and artificial lubrication, potentially increasing the risk of tearing and other skin damage. In other worlds it is not a normal practice among the most civilized people of the ancient world governed by Alllah's way of life.

Questions to think about: *Of course age and life experiences may limit how one understands and accepts the way of life Alllah set forth for us living in the current Adamic civilization ruled under "white privilege".*

- Why has Alllah asked husbands and wife's to keep His way of suitability for sexual intercourse by waiting for the womb of the women to complete menstruation or purification?
- What is a savage?

Quran Reminder Concerning Proper Business Ethics

14. "Woe to the cheaters! Who, when they take the measure (*of their dues*) from men, take it fully, And when they measure out to others or weigh out for them, they give less than is due. Do they not think that they will be raised again, To a mighty day? --The day when men will stand before the Lord of the worlds. Nay, surely the record of the wicked is in the prison. And what will make thee know what the prison is? It is a written book." (Holy Quran Chapter 83)

15. "Do not usurp one another's property by unjust means, nor offer it to the judges (as bribe) so that you may devour knowingly and unjustly a portion of the goods of others." (Holy Quran Chapter 2 verse 188)

16. "O you who have believed! Do not devour one anothers property by unlawful ways; but do business with mutual consent." (Holy Quran Chapter 4 verse 29)

17. "And O my people! Give just measure and weight, nor withhold from the people the things that are their due: commit not evil in the land with intent to do mischief." (Holy Quran Chapter 11 verse 85)

- Are you a cheating business person?
- How could the U.S. housing crisis of 2007 have been avoided if Holy Quran 4:29 was applied by Wall Street, The Federal Reserve and the U.S. Government Regulators?
- Is foreclosure usurping another person's property by unlawful means according to Islamic law?
- Why do corporate executives earn 10 to 20 times more than average employees and how can the Holy Quran fix this problem of cheating and unethical business practices?

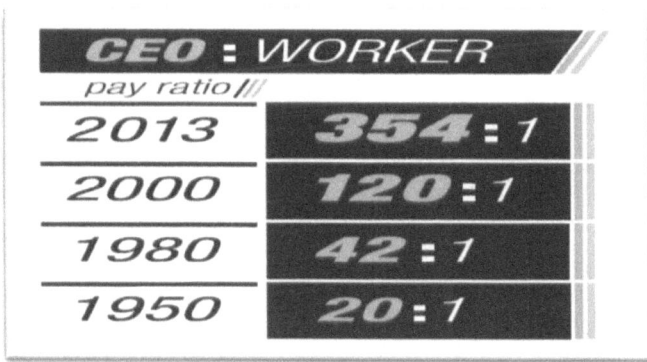

Quranic Reminder Concerning Good Food

18. "Forbidden to you is that which dies of itself, and blood, and flesh of swine, and that on which any other name than that of Allah has been invoked, and the strangled (animal), and that

beaten to death, and that killed by a fall, and that killed by goring with the horn, and that which wild beasts have eaten -- except what you slaughter; and that which is sacrificed on stones set up (for idols), and that you seek to divide by arrows; that is a transgression. This day have those who disbelieve despaired of your religion, so fear them not, and fear Me. This day have I perfected for you your religion and completed My favour to you and chosen for you Islam as a religion. But whoever is compelled by hunger, not including willfully to sin, then surely Allah is Forgiving, merciful. They ask thee as to what is allowed them. Say: The good things are allowed to you, and what you have taught the beasts and birds of prey, training them to hunt -- you teach them of what Allah has taught you; so eat of that which they catch for you and mention the name of Allah over it; and keep your duty to Allah. Surely Allah is Swift in reckoning." (Holy Quran Chapter 5 verses 3-4)

Questions to think about: *Of course age and life experiences may limit how one understands and accepts the way of life Alllah set forth for us living in the current Adamic civilization ruled under "white privilege".*

- Do you eat swine, why?

- Why does Alllah forbid the righteous from eating pork and animals killed in the worst manner, except in times of great hunger?
- Why is it that Alllah is even concerned about what you and I eat?

Quranic Reminder Concerning the Love of this Worlds Life of Materialism i.e. Caucasian Gross Materialism

19. "Fair-seeming to men is made the love of desires, of women and sons and hoarded treasures of gold and silver and well-bred horses and cattle and tilth (fields). This is the provision of the life of this world. And Allah — with Him is the good goal (of life)." (Holy Quran Chapter 3 verse 13)

20. "Those who love this world's life more than the Hereafter, and turn away from Allah's path, and would have it crooked. Those are far astray."
(Holy Quran Chapter 14 verse 3)

21. "Whoso disbelieves in Allah after his belief — not he who is compelled while his heart is content with faith, but he who opens (his) breast for disbelief — on them is the wrath of Allah, and for them is a grievous chastisement. That is because they love this world's life more than the Hereafter, and because Allah guides not the disbelieving people." (Holy Quran Chapter 16 verse 106-107)

22. "Surely We have revealed the Qur'an to thee, in portions. So wait patiently for the judgment of thy Lord, and obey not a sinner or an ungrateful one

among them. And glorify the name of thy Lord morning and evening. And during part of the night adore Him, and glorify Him throughout a long night. Surely these love the transitory life and neglect a grievous day before them. We created them and made firm their make, and, when We will, We can bring in their place the like of them by change. Surely this is a Reminder; so whoever will, let him take a way to his Lord." (Holy Quran Chapter 76 verse 23-27)

23. "By those running and uttering cries! And those producing fire, striking! And those suddenly attacking at morn! Then thereby they raise dust, Then penetrate thereby gatherings. Surely man is ungrateful to his Lord. And surely he is a witness of that. And truly on account of the love of wealth he is niggardly. Knows he not when that which is in the graves is raised, And that which is in the breasts is made manifest? Surely their Lord this day is Aware of them." (Holy Quran Chapter 100 verse 1-11)

__Questions to think about:__ *Of course age and life experiences may limit how one understands and accepts the way of life Alllah set forth for us living in the current Adamic civilization ruled under "white privilege".*

- Why did Alllah permit (make) the white race to be firm in ruling, for a short time, as greedy rulers on earth?
- What means have you gone to acquire material gain, beget children and attract women or men, why or why not?
- Who do you know prosecuting wars, attacking nations, forming allies to steal wealth, such as oil, gold minds, and minerals?
- What is being niggardly mean?

Quranic Reminder Concerning Love Between Men and Women

24. "And of His signs is this, that He created mates for you from yourselves that you might find quiet of mind in them, and He put between you love and compassion. Surely there are signs in this for a people who reflect." (Holy Quran Chapter 30 verse 21)

- Since Alllah put love and compassion between mates, what type of divine force is it that attracts couples?
- What has kept you attracted to your mate?

Quranic Reminder Concerning Choosing Friendships

25. "O you who believe, take not My enemy and your enemy for friends. Would you offer them love, while they deny the Truth that has come to you, driving out the Messenger and yourselves because you believe in Allah, your Lord? If you have come forth to strive in My way and to seek My pleasure, would you love them in secret? And I know what you conceal and what you manifest. And whoever of you does this, he indeed strays from the straight path. If they overcome you, they will be your enemies, and will stretch forth their hands and their tongues towards you with evil, and they desire that you may disbelieve. Your relationships and your children would not profit you, on the day of Resurrection — He will decide between you. And Allah is Seer of what you do." (Holy Quran Chapter 60 verses 1-3)

- How many thought your friendships made with influential members of the white race from 1963 to present time is true?
- Has such friendships based upon political, socio-economic interest, benefited you and your children up to present times?
- The Holy Quran 60:2 says, *"If they overcome you, they will be your enemies, and will stretch forth their hands and their tongues towards you with evil".* How does this verse relate to you or the relationship between blacks and Jews (whites in general) in North America?

Quranic Reminder Concerning Women Who Accept Islam As A Way Of Life

26. "O you who have believed, when the believing women come to you as emigrants, examine and test (*their faith*), although Allah only knows best the truth of their faith. Then, when you find them to be true believers, do not return them to the disbelievers. Neither are they lawful for the disbelievers nor are the disbelievers lawful for them. Return to their disbelieving husbands the dowers that they had given them; and there is no blame on you if you marry them when you have paid them their dowers. And you also should not hold back unbelieving women in marriage. Ask for the dowers that you had given to your unbelieving wives, and let the disbelievers ask for the dowers that they had given to their Muslim wives. This is Allah's command: He judges between you, and He is All-Knowing, All-Wise. And if you do not get back from the disbelievers a part of the dower of your disbelieving wives, and then your turn comes, pay to the people whose wives

have been left on the other side an amount equivalent to the dowers given by them. And fear that Allah in Whom you have believed." (Holy Quran Chapter verse 10-11)

Questions to think about: *Of course age and life experiences may limit how one understands and accepts the way of life Alllah set forth for us living in the current Adamic civilization ruled under "white privilege".*

- Should a Muslim man marry a women who believe does not believe in Alllah?
- How do you know if your spouse believes in Alllah or disbelieves in Alllah's way of life?
- If a Muslim women returns to disbelief in Alllah after believing, can she marry a man whom also does not believe in Alllah's way of life?
- Should a Muslim woman marry a disbelieving man?

Quranic Reminder Concerning Gossip Media and Misleading Frivolous Conversation

27. Those who *love* to see scandal published broadcast among the Believers, will have a grievous Penalty in this life and in the Hereafter: Allah knows, and ye know not. (Holy Quran 24:19)
28. "And of men is he who takes instead frivolous discourse to lead astray from Allah's path without knowledge, and to make it a mockery. For such is an abasing chastisement. And when Our messages are recited to him, he turns back proudly, as if he had not heard them, as if there were deafness in his ears; so announce to him a

painful chastisement. (Holy Quran Chapter 31 verses 6-7)

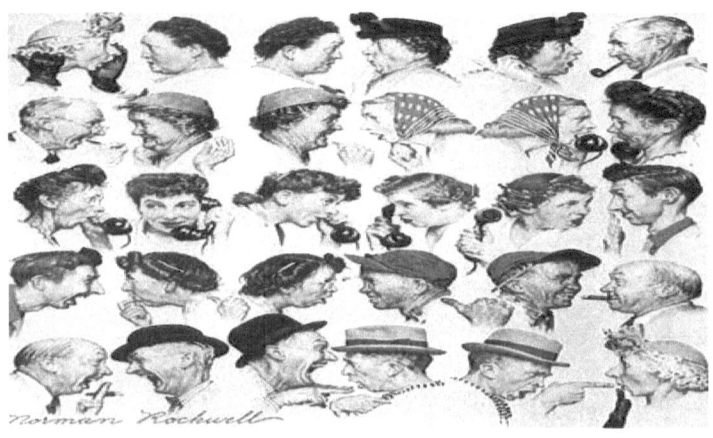

Questions to think about: *Of course age and life experiences may limit how one understands and accepts the way of life Alllah set forth for us living in the current Adamic civilization ruled under "white privilege".*

- Do you love reading published scandals or broadcast?
- Do you write gossip on social media?
- Can you name a few gossip column and name who finances any?
- How does Alllah want to handle scandal media and people who take unwise frivolous conversation to mislead others into wrong doing?
- How will Islam be applied to clean up gossip and frivolous discourse?
- Is gossiping a form of networking in Islam, Christianity or any other religion?

Quranic Reminder Concerning Homosexuality

29. "Do you come to the males from among the creatures, And leave your wives whom your Lord has created for you? Nay, you are a people exceeding limits." (Holy Quran Chapter 26 verses 165-166)

30. "Will you come to men lustfully rather than women? Nay, you are a people who act ignorantly!" (Holy Quran Chapter 27 verses 55)

Questions to think about: *Of course age and life experiences may limit how one understands and accepts the way of life Alllah set forth for us living in the current Adamic civilization ruled under "white privilege".*

- How do you feel about homosexuality as it is promoted under white privilege's social order?
- Why are men having sex with men or women doing the same with women considered exceeding limits (the final, utmost, or furthest boundary or point as to extent, amount, continuance, procedure, etc.)?
- Why does Alllah—The God of the Original Black Nation say homosexuality is acting ignorantly—unaware of its long-term side

effects to certain parts of the body and society in general?
- What is sodomy?

Quranic Reminder Concerning The Wives of Prophets

31. "O wives of the Prophet, whoever of you is guilty of manifestly improper conduct, the chastisement will be doubled for her. And this is easy for Allah. And stay in your houses and display not (your beauty) like the displaying of the ignorance of old; and keep up prayer, and pay the poor-rate, and obey Allah and His Messenger. Allah only desires to take away uncleanness from you, O people of the household, and to purify you a (thorough) purifying. And remember that which is recited in your houses of the messages of Allah and the Wisdom. Surely Allah is ever Knower of subtleties, Aware. (Holy Quran Chapter 33 verses 33-34)

__Questions to think about:__ Of course age and life experiences may limit how one understands and accepts the way of life Alllah set forth for us living in the current Adamic civilization ruled under "white privilege".

- What do you consider improper sexual conduct by any women married?
- Does Alllah mean for women to stay in their houses forever?
- What is the difference between women displaying her beauty righteously as opposed to displaying her "booty" and everything in as seen throughout the

streets of nearly every between throughout most commercial cities and towns worldwide?

- Why does Alllah want certain people "extra clean" to represent His message to the public?

Quranic Reminder Concerning Warfare—Self Defense and Cessation of War

32. O you who believe, retaliation is prescribed for you in the matter of the slain: the free for the free, and the slave for the slave, and the female for the female. But if remission is made to one by his (aggrieved) brother, prosecution (for blood-money) should be according to usage, and payment to him in a good manner. This is an alleviation from your Lord and a mercy. Whoever exceeds the limit after this, will have a painful chastisement. And there is life for you in retaliation, O men of understanding, that you may guard yourselves. (Holy Quran Chapter 2 verse 178)

33. "And fight in the way of Allah against those who fight against you but be not aggressive. Surely Allah loves not the aggressors. And kill them wherever you find them, and drive them out from where they drove you out, and persecution is worse than slaughter. And fight not with them at the Sacred Mosque until they fight with you in it; so if they fight you (in it), slay them. Such is the recompense of the disbelievers. But if they desist, then surely Allah is Forgiving, Merciful. And fight them until there is no persecution, and religion is

only for Allah. But if they desist, then there should be no hostility except against the oppressors. (Holy Quran Chapter 2 verses 190-193)

Questions to think about: *Of course age and life experiences may limit how one understands and accepts the way of life Alllah set forth for us living in the current Adamic civilization ruled under "white privilege".*

- Have you ever retaliated against someone who tried to harm you or family members?
- Have you ever felt like retaliating against others for murdering someone close to you?
- Why does Alllah permit killing the aggressors?
- Why is persecution worse than slaughter?
- When should all fighting stop during warfare?
- When have you ever turned your other cheat to be slapped by someone trying to hurt you?

Quranic Reminder Concerning Match Making For Couples

34. "Surely the men who submit and the women who submit, and the believing men and the believing women, and the obeying men and the obeying women, and the truthful men and the truthful women, and the patient men and the patient women, and the humble men and the humble women, and the charitable men and the charitable women, and the fasting men and the fasting women, and the men who guard their chastity and the women who guard, and the men who remember Allah

much and women who remember — Allah has prepared for them forgiveness and a mighty reward. And it behoves not a believing man or a believing woman, when Allah and His Messenger have decided an affair, to exercise a choice in their matter. And whoever disobeys Allah and His Messenger, he surely strays off to manifest error." (Holy Quran Chapter 33 verses 35-36)

Questions to think about: *Of course age and life experiences may limit how one understands and accepts the way of life Alllah set forth for us living in the current Adamic civilization ruled under "white privilege".*

- What are the number 1 and 2 reasons you have not found a mate or remained with your mate?
- Had any of your relationship failures been due to lack of the common denominators such as those mentioned in Holy Quran 33:35-36?
- What makes believing men and believing women best matches?

Quranic Reminder Concerning The Caucasian Jews, Christians and Sabians (Middle Eastern tradition)

35. "Surely those who believe, and those who are Jews, and the Christians, and the Sabians,

whoever believes in Allah and the Last Day and does good, they have their reward with their Lord, and there is no fear for them, nor shall they grieve. And when <u>We made a covenant with you and raised the mountain above you</u>: Hold fast that which We have given you, and bear in mind what is in it, so that you may guard against evil. Then after that you turned back; and had it not been for the grace of Allah and His mercy on you, you had certainly been among the losers. And indeed you know those among you who violated the Sabbath, so We said to them: Be (as) apes, despised and hated. So We made them an example to those who witnessed it and those who came after it and an admonition to those who guard against evil." (Holy Quran Chapter 2 verses 62-66)

*I have underlines the verse *"We made a covenant with you and raised the mountain above you"*…because this verse actually refers to a time 6,000 plus year ago when the Caucasian race dwelled in the hills and caves sides of Europe's Caucus Mountains. According to the teachings of the Most Honorable Elijah Muhammad, the Caucasians who first let loose from the caves were called Jews. And, with what they were taught 4,000 years ago by Musa (Moses)—which led them out of Europe's Caucus Mountain Range—rather than teach the rest of their western brethren (gentiles), they hid Moses' book, thus leaving the gentiles back for thousands of years in savagery and barbarity. Later in time, Jews were hated by their western brethren throughout all of Europe. *The "ape comment" mentioned by our ancestors in Quran 5:60;* **"They are those whom Allah has cursed and upon whom He brought His wrath and of whom He made apes and swine, and who serve the devil"** informs the entire world what *occurred 6,000 years ago in the caves of Europe. In brief, the worst of them began mating with animals, this we have apes so says the Honorable Elijah Muhammad and the reason the rulers of the white race hid Quran from her former black slaves. But I digress.*

> 36. "The likeness of those who were charged with the Torah, then they observed it not, is as the likeness of the ass carrying books. Evil is the likeness of the people who reject the messages of Allah. And Allah guides not the iniquitous people."

37. Say: O People of the Book, do you find fault with us for aught except that we believe in Allah and in that which has been revealed to us and that which was revealed before, while most of you are transgressors? Say: Shall I inform you of those worse than this in retribution from Allah? They are those whom Allah has cursed and upon whom He brought His wrath and of whom He made apes and swine, and who serve the devil. These are in a worse plight and further astray from the straight path." (Holy Quran Chapter 5 verses 59-60)

38. "So when they neglected that whereof they had been reminded, We delivered those who forbade evil and We overtook those who were iniquitous with an evil chastisement because they transgressed. So when they revoltingly persisted in that which they had been forbidden, We said to them: Be (as) apes, despised and hated. And when thy Lord declared that He would send against them to the day of Resurrection those who would subject them to severe torment. Surely thy Lord is Quick in requiting; and surely He is Forgiving, Merciful. And We divided them in the earth into parties — some of them are righteous and some of them are otherwise. And We tried them with blessings and misfortunes that they might turn. Then after them came an evil posterity who inherited the Book, taking the frail goods of this low life and saying: It will be forgiven us. And if the like good came to them, they would take it (too). Was not a promise taken from them in the Book that they would not speak anything about Allah but the truth? And they study what is in it. And the abode of the Hereafter is better for those who keep their duty. Do you not then understand?" (Holy Quran Chapter 7 verses 165-169)

*The word Jews appears 14 times in the Quran. The verses underlined above foretold in advance how two types of Jews were divided into two parties. The Orthodox Jews were first and the Zionist Jews came second. The founders of Zionism are known today as the European Jews of Germany. One of the most powerful families of these two parties are named Rothschild. Of course, there are other families in America and Vatican city, but suffice it to say, of these parties i.e., Orthodox Jews and Zionist Jews Alllah knew well in advance. He knew an evil posterity from them would inherit the book and wealth for a short time so says the Holy Quran 7:168: *"And We divided them throughout the earth into nations. Of them some were righteous, and of them some were otherwise. And We tested them with good [times] and bad that perhaps they would return [to obedience]."*

The Rothschild family combined with the Dutch House of Orange to found Bank of Amsterdam in the early 1600's as the world's first private central bank. Prince William of Orange married into the English House of Windsor, taking King James II's daughter Mary as his bride. The Orange Order Brotherhood, which more recently fomented Northern Ireland Protestant violence, put William III on the English throne where he ruled both Holland and Britain. In 1694 William III teamed up with the Rothschild's to launch the Bank of England.[7]

37. "And We have revealed to thee the Book with the truth, verifying that which is before it of the Book and a guardian over it, so judge between them by what Allah has revealed, and follow not their low desires, (turning away) from the truth that has come to thee. For everyone of you We

[7] http://topinfopost.com/2013/07/10/the-house-of-rothschild

appointed a law and a way. And if Allah had pleased He would have made you a single people, but that He might try you in what He gave you. So vie one with another in virtuous deeds. To Allah you will all return, so He will inform you of that wherein you differed; And that thou shouldst judge between them by what Allah has revealed, and follow not their low desires, and be cautious of them lest they seduce thee from part of what Allah has revealed to thee. Then if they turn away, know that Allah desires to afflict them for some of their sins. And surely many of the people are transgressors. Is it then the judgment of ignorance that they desire? And who is better than Allah to judge for a people who are sure? O you who believe, take not the Jews and the Christians for friends. They are friends of each other. And whoever amongst you takes them for friends he is indeed one of them. Surely Allah guides not the unjust people." (Holy Quran Chapter 5 verses 48-51)

**Questions to think about:** _Of course age and life experiences may limit how one understands and accepts the way of life Alllah set forth for us living in the current Adamic civilization ruled under "white privilege"._

- What does friend really mean in Quran, does it mean help and comfort?
- Does Zionist control the central banks of Europe and America?
- Does Zionist control Hollywood and the Oscars?
- Does Zionist control Negro leaders in North America?
- Does Zionist control the Federal Reserve Bank in Washington DC?
- What is a Zionist, when did they come to power?

- What divine writ does Zionist apply to govern this world order?
- What is the difference between the NETUREI KARTA Orthodox Jews and Zionist Jews?
- What is a European Jew?
- What is a Semitic Jew?
- What is a Zionist Jew?

Neturei Karta Orthodox Jews who met with Hon. Min. Farrakhan

Zionist Jews who oppose to meet with Hon. Min. Farrakhan

Quranic Reminder Concerning How To Fight Off Evil Thoughts

38. "If a suggestion from Satan assail thy (mind), seek refuge with Allah; for He heareth and knoweth (all things). Those who fear Allah, when a thought of evil from Satan assaults them, bring Allah to remembrance, when lo! they see (aright)! But their brethren (the evil ones) plunge them deeper into error, and never relax (their efforts). If thou bring them not a revelation, they say: "Why hast thou not got it together?" Say: *"I but follow what is revealed to me from my Lord: this is (nothing but) Lights from your Lord, and Guidance,*

and Mercy, for any who have faith." When the Quran is read, listen to it with attention, and hold your peace that you may receive Mercy."
(Holy Quran Chapter 7 verses 200-204)

<u>Questions to think about:</u> *Of course age and life experiences may limit how one understands and accepts the way of life Alllah set forth for us living in the current Adamic civilization ruled under "white privilege".*

- How do you counter those thoughts that attempt to bring down spirit or attitude into depression?
- Do you read the Quran or even listen to the Quran daily or at least once a week?
- How do you describe Satan attacking or making suggestions within your mind?

Quranic Reminder Concerning Peace Among Brethern, Laughing at Others, Fault Finding In Your Own People, Nick-Names, Avoiding Most Suspicion, Spying and Backbiting

39. The believers are brethren so make peace between your brethren, and keep your duty to Allah that mercy may be had on you. O you who believe, let not people laugh at people, perchance they may be better than they; nor let women (laugh) at women, perchance they may be better than they. Neither find fault with your own people, nor call one another by nick-names. Evil is a bad name after faith; and whoso turns not, these it is that are the iniquitous. O you who believe,

avoid most of suspicion, for surely suspicion in some cases is sin; and spy not nor let some of you backbite others. Does one of you like to eat the flesh of his dead brother? You abhor it! And keep your duty to Allah, surely Allah is Oft-returning (to mercy), Merciful.

Questions to think about: *Of course age and life experiences may limit how one understands and accepts the way of life Alllah set forth for us living in the current Adamic civilization ruled under "white privilege".*

- Do you go to war against your Muslims brothers?
- How do you feel when others make fun of you?
- Do women laugh at the manner in which other women dress, Why?
- Do you oft-times seek to find fault in people?
- Do you spy-on people and backbite others as Alllah says not too, why should we abhor it?
- Do you write and speak in ambiguous terms against Minister Louis Farrakhan? What is really in your heart or mind against him?

Quranic Reminder Concerning Lending Money and Collecting Debt

40. "O you who believe, keep your duty to Allah and relinquish what remains (due) from usury, if you are believers. But if you do (it) not, then be apprised of war from Allah and His Messenger; and if you repent, then you shall have your capital. Wrong not, and you shall not be wronged. And if (the debtor) is in straitness, let there be postponement till (he is in) ease. And that you remit (it) as alms is better for you, if you only knew." (Holy Quran Chapter 2 verses 278-280)

Questions to think about: *Of course age and life experiences may limit how one understands and accepts the way of life Alllah set forth for us living in the current Adamic civilization ruled under "white privilege".*

- What is usury: *an unconscionable or exorbitant rate or amount of interest;* specifically: *interest in excess of a legal rate charged to a borrower for the use of money)* and how does it ruin entire economies?

- Why does Alllah tell the Islamic people to relinquish what remains of usury and to remit (return money) debt as a gift for people suffering during hard times?

Quranic Reminder Concerning Trade

41. "O you who believe, devour not your property among yourselves by illegal methods except that it be trading by your mutual consent. And kill not your people. Surely Allah is ever Merciful to you. And whoso does this aggressively and unjustly, We shall soon cast him into fire. And this is ever easy for Allah. If you shun the great things which you are forbidden, We shall do away with your evil (inclinations) and cause you to enter an honorable place of entering. And covet not that by which Allah has made some of you excel others. For men is the benefit of what they earn. And for women is the benefit of what they earn. And ask Allah of His grace. Surely Allah is ever Knower of all things." (Holy Quran Chapter 4 verses 29-32)

Questions to think about: *Of course age and life experiences may limit how one understands and accepts the way of life Alllah set forth for us living in the current Adamic civilization ruled under "white privilege".*

- How does one devour the property of others by illegal methods?
- What is trading by mutual consent?
- Do you have any inclinations to devour, by illegal

methods, the benefits from someone that has earned their keep?

- Have you ever cheated someone out of money, for what and why?

Quranic Reminder Concerning Adultery, Lewd Acts, Killing Children, Stealing Money from Orphans

42. "Surely the chastisement of their Lord is (a thing) not to be felt secure from —And those who restrain their sexual passions, Except in the presence of their mates or those whom their right hands possess — for such surely are not to be blamed, But he who seeks to go beyond this, these are the transgressors. (Holy Quran Chapter 70 verse 29)

43. "And they who call not upon another god with Allah and slay not the soul which Allah has forbidden, except in the cause of justice, nor commit fornication; and he who does this shall meet a requital of sin —" (Holy Quran Chapter 26 verse 68)

44. "Say: Come! I will recite what your Lord has forbidden to you: Associate naught with Him and do good to parents and slay not your children for (fear of) poverty — We provide for you and for them — and draw not nigh to indecencies, open or secret, and kill not the soul which Allah has made sacred except in the course of justice. This He enjoins upon you that you may understand. And approach not the property of the orphan except in the best manner, until he attains his maturity. And give full measure and weight with equity — We impose not on any soul a duty except to the extent of its ability. And when you speak, be just, though it be (against) a relative. And fulfill Allah's covenant. This He enjoins on you that you may be mindful; And (know) that this is My path, the right one, so follow it, and follow not (other) ways, for they will lead you away from His way. This He enjoins on you that you may keep your duty." (Holy Quran Chapter Verses 151-153)

Questions to think about: _Of course age and life experiences may limit how one understands and accepts the way of life Alllah set forth for us living in the current Adamic civilization ruled under "white privilege"._

- How many of you heard of foster parents stealing money from their foster children
- How many times have you committed fornication in secret or public?
- How many people have been executed in prison unjustly?
- Does adultery lead to Murder, why?

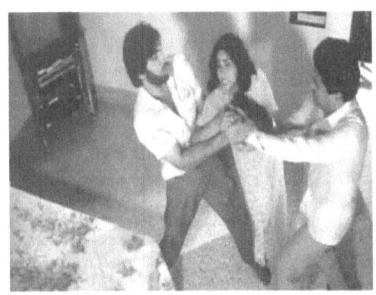 

- Can applying the Holy Quran's way of life correct these social problems, if yes, how?

Quranic Reminder Concerning How to Act And To Speak

45. "And turn not thy face away from people in contempt, nor go about in the land exultingly. Surely Allah loves not any self-conceited boaster. And pursue the right course in thy going about and lower thy voice. Surely the most hateful of voices is braying of asses. See you not that Allah has made subservient to you whatever is in the heavens and whatever is in the earth, and granted to you His favours complete outwardly and inwardly? And among men is he who disputes concerning Allah without knowledge or guidance or a Book giving light." (Holy Quran Chapter 31 verses 18-20)

FACE OF CONTEMPT

46. "And say to My servants that they speak what is best. Surely the devil sows dissensions among them. The devil is surely an open enemy to man. Your Lord knows you best. He will have mercy on you, if He please, or He will chastise you, if He please. And We have not sent thee as being in charge of them." (Holy Quran Chapter 17 verses 53-54)

Questions to think about: _Of course age and life experiences may limit how one understands and accepts the way of life Alllah set forth for us living in the current Adamic civilization ruled under "white privilege"._

- How do feel about a loud mouth person always boasting, is this not a hateful voice?
- Has anyone looked at you with a face of contempt (scorn as if you were worthless) and turned away?
- Do you know men and women who dispute concerning _Alllah_ using ignorance, without knowledge or reading the Book of Psalms?
- Who has rights in Islam being in charge over another human being?

Quranic Reminder Concerning Proper Treatment of Slaves

47. "And marry those among you who are single, and those who are fit among your male slaves and your female slaves. If they are needy, Allah will make them free from want out of His grace. And Allah is Ample-giving, Knowing. And let those who cannot find a match keep chaste, until Allah makes them free from want out of His grace. And those of your slaves who ask for a writing (of freedom), give them the writing, if you know any

good in them, and give them of the wealth of Allah which He has given you. And compel not your slave-girls to prostitution when they desire to keep chaste, in order to seek the frail goods of this world's life. And whoever compels them, then surely after their compulsion Allah is Forgiving, Merciful." (Holy Quran Chapter 24 verses 32-33)

Questions to think about: *Of course age and life experiences may limit how one understands and accepts the way of life Alllah set forth for us living in the current Adamic civilization ruled under "white privilege".*

- How many women, men, young boys and girls prostitute themselves seeking the frail goods of this world's life?
- Why does Alllah forgive and show mercy to people if they are forced into prostitution?
- How do you feel about black people being slaves in Pre-Islamic and post Islam Arabia and Christian America?

*Old world Islamic sharia law accepted (and accepts) slavery, as did other legal systems of ancient times such as Roman law, Hebrew law, Byzantine Christian law, African customary law and Hindu law.

The world was very different in those days, and practices that seem profoundly unethical to modern minds were common and accepted.[8]

8

http://www.bbc.co.uk/religion/religions/islam/history/slavery_1.shtml

48. "And what will make thee comprehend what the uphill road is? (It is) to free a slave, Or to feed in a day of hunger An orphan nearly related, Or the poor man lying in the dust. Then he is of those who believe and exhort one another to patience, and exhort one another to mercy. These are the people of the right hand. And those who disbelieve in Our messages, they are the people of the left hand. On them is Fire closed over." (Holy Quran Chapter 90 verses 12-20)

  *The word slave means: *a person who is the property of and wholly subject to another; a bond servant.*

- How does anyone become a slave under another person, in a town, a city or a country?
- Why would any man or government in the case of America enslave anyone; how does economics play into slave labor?
- Why would Alllah—God permit Christians of America to enslave other men or women?
- According to Quran, how is Alllah ultimately going to eradicate slave masters and selfish people?

Quranic Reminder Concerning Alcohol, Intoxicants, Gambling and Cleanliness before Prayer

49. "O you who believe, go not near prayer when you are intoxicated till you know what you say, nor after sexual intercourse — except you are merely passing by — until you have bathed. And if you are sick, or on a journey, or one of you come from the privy, or you have touched the women, and you cannot find water, betake yourselves to pure earth, then wipe your faces and your hands. Surely Allah is ever Pardoning, Forgiving." (Holy Quran Chapter 4 verse 43)

50. "O you who believe, intoxicants and games of chance and (sacrificing to) stones set up and (dividing by) arrows are only an uncleanness, the devil's work; so shun it that you may succeed. The devil desires only to create enmity and hatred among you by means of intoxicants and games of chance, and to keep you back from the remembrance of Allah and from prayer. Will you then keep back? And obey Allah and obey the Messenger and be cautious. But if you turn back then know that the duty of Our Messenger is only a clear deliverance of the message.

51. "They ask thee about intoxicants and games of chance. Say: In both of them is a great sin and (some) advantage for men, and their sin is greater than their advantage. And they ask thee as to what the they should spend. Say: What you can spare. Thus does Allah make clear to you the messages that you may ponder," (Holy Quran Chapter 2 verse 219)

Questions to think about: *Of course age and life experiences may limit how one understands and accepts the way of life Alllah set forth for us living in the current Adamic civilization ruled under "white privilege".*

- In the early stages of Islamic life, Muslims drank wine, but later Alllah forbade it altogether, true or false? If true why?
- Muslims must clean themselves with if water is not available?
- Is playing the lottery (numbers) games of chance and do you play from time to time hoping to win big?
- How does intoxicants and gambling create hatred among people who get involved in it?

Quranic Reminder for People Pray And Do Good

52. "Allah chooses messengers from angels and from men. Surely Allah is Hearing, Seeing. He knows what is before them and what is behind them. And to Allah are all affairs returned. O you who believe, bow down and prostrate yourselves and serve your Lord, and do good that you may

succeed. And strive hard for Allah with due striving. He has chosen you and has not laid upon you any hardship in religion — the faith of your father Abraham. He named you Muslims before and in this, that the Messenger may be a bearer of witness to you, and you may be bearers of witness to the people; so keep up prayer and pay the poor-rate and hold fast to Allah. He is your Protector; excellent the Protector and excellent the Helper!" (Holy Quran Chapter 22 verse 75-78)

Questions to think about: _Of course age and life experiences may limit how one understands and accepts the way of life Alllah set forth for us living in the current Adamic civilization ruled under "white privilege"._

- Why does Alllah want us to Pray and do good to succeed?
- Can men be messengers of God, how about a black man in North America?
- Why does Allah say He is our protector and an excellent helper?
- What is the poor-rate in Islam and how does it help and Islamic governments operational needs?

Quranic Reminder How to Enter Someone's Home, Burglarly Prohibited

53. "O you who believe, enter not houses other than your own houses, until you have asked permission and saluted those in them. This is better for you that you may be mindful. But if you find no one therein, enter them not, until permission is given to you; and if it is said to you, Go back, then go back; this is purer for you. And

Allah is Knower of what you do. It is no sin for you to enter uninhabited houses wherein you have your necessaries. And Allah knows what you do openly and what you hide." (Holy Quran Chapter 24 verse 27-29)

Questions to think about: *Of course age and life experiences may limit how one understands and accepts the way of life Alllah set forth for us living in the current Adamic civilization ruled under "white privilege".*

- Why does Alllah Say "O you who believe?
- Is burglary a crime in Islam?
- When is it permissible to enter the house of other people?

Quranic Reminder that Caucasians and/or Zionist Jews Have no Power over Black People

54. "O you that believe! fear Allah and believe in His apostle and He will bestow on you a double portion of His Mercy: He will provide for you a light by which ye shall walk (straight in your path) and He will forgive you (your past): For Allah is Oft-Forgiving. Most Merciful:

That the <u>People of the Book</u> may know that they have no power whatever over the Grace of Allah that (His) Grace is (entirely) in his hand to bestow it on whomsoever He wills. For Allah is the Lord of Grace abounding" (Holy Quran Chapter 57 verses 28-29)

Questions to think about: *Of course age and life experiences may limit how one understands and accepts the way of life Alllah set forth for us living in the current Adamic civilization ruled under "white privilege".*

- Who are the People of the Book as shown underlined in passage above?
- Why did Alllah offer to forgive the descendants of former America's slaves, their past ill actions, once they (we) believe, fear Him (Alllah) and believe in His Apostle?
- What is Grace?
- Why do white people angrily think they or the US America helps Black people more than God?

Quranic Reminders Concerning Polygamy, Multiplying Families, Culture and Sharing Wealth of the Family Wealth

4:1 "O people, keep your duty to your Lord, Who created you from a single being and created its mate of the same (kind), and spread from these two many men and women. And keep your duty to Allah, by Whom you demand one of another (your rights), and (to) the ties of relationship. Surely Allah is ever a Watcher over you.

4:2 And give to the orphans their property, and substitute not worthless (things) for (their) good (ones), and devour not their property (adding) to your own property. This is surely a great sin.

4:3 And if you fear that you cannot do justice to orphans, marry such women as seem good to you, two, or three, or four; but if you fear that you will not do justice, then (marry) only one or that which your right hands possess. This is more proper that you may not do injustice.

4:4 And give women their dowries as a free gift. But if they of themselves be pleased to give you a portion thereof, consume it with enjoyment and pleasure.

4:5 And make not over your property, which Allah has made a (means of) support for you, to the weak of understanding, and maintain them out of it, and clothe them and give them a good education.

4:6 And test the orphans until they reach the age of marriage. Then if you find in them maturity of intellect, make over to them their property, and consume it not extravagantly and hastily against their growing up. And whoever is rich, let him abstain, and whoever is poor let him consume reasonably. And when you make over to them their property, call witnesses in their presence. And Allah is enough as a Reckoner.

4:7 For men is a share of what the parents and the near relatives leave, and for women a share of what the parents and the near relatives leave, whether it be little or much — an appointed share. (Holy Quran Chapter 4 verses 4-7)

Questions to think about: _Of course age and life experiences may limit how one understands and accepts the way of life Alllah set forth for us living in the current Adamic civilization ruled under "white privilege"._

- How many men decide not marry a single woman with several children, why?
- How many men have "*you*" slept with hoping to keep a husband or good boyfriend?
- How many women have "*you*" slept with hoping to find a wife or good girlfriend?
- Why does Alllah say one wife is best if you fear you cannot do justice---*fair dealing*—by more than one wife?
- Why do men and women have random sex or multiple boyfriends or girlfriends?
- Why does Alllah say maintain those with weak understanding and educate them and provided for them out of how you earn a living?
- How does Alllah lay a foundation for building families and wealth in Holy Quran 4:1 and 4:7?

Recommended Reading: Guide to Understanding Bible and Quran